D1518877

How to Draw Cartoon Symbols of the Wild West

Curt Visca and Kelley Visca

The Rosen Publishing Group's

PowerKids Press™

New York

Dedicated to our son, Clark, our newest little buckaroo

Published in 2004 by The Rosen Publishing Group, Inc.
29 East 21st Street, New York, NY 10010

First Edition

Editor: Natashya Wilson
Book Design: Kim Sonsky
Layout Design: Michael J. Caroleo

Illustration Credits: All illustrations © Curt Visca.
Photo Credits: Cover and p. 6 © Ray Hendley/Index Stock Imagery, Inc.; p. 8 © Vince Streano/CORBIS; pp. 10, 16 © Phil Schermeister/CORBIS; p. 12 © Joseph Sohm; Visions of America/CORBIS; p. 14 Annie Griffiths Belt/CORBIS; p. 18 © Henry Diltz/CORBIS; p. 20 © SuperStock.

Visca, Curt.
How to draw cartoon symbols of the wild west / Curt Visca and Kelley Visca.— 1st ed.
    v. cm. — (A kid's guide to drawing)
Includes bibliographical references and index.
Contents: Cartoon symbols of the wild west — American bison — Railroad — The Pony Express — Conestoga wagon — Native American tepee — Cowboy — Marshal — The gold rush.
ISBN 0-8239-6728-X
1. West (U.S.)—In art—Juvenile literature. 2. Drawing—Technique—Juvenile literature. [1. West (U.S.)—In art. 2. Cartooning—Technique. 3. Drawing—Technique.] I. Visca, Kelley. II. Title. III. Series.
NC655 .V583 2004
741.5—dc21
                                        2002010543

Manufactured in the United States of America

CONTENTS

Cartoon Symbols of the Wild West

In the mid-1800s, **pioneers** traveled across the Mississippi River to the western **frontier** in covered wagons. They searched for land, gold, and adventure. Some pioneers had to deal with wild animals, bad weather, and even bandits. The western frontier came to be called the Wild West. Many of the pioneers were farmers. Doctors, shopkeepers, blacksmiths, and others also set out to find **opportunities** for a new life. When the California gold rush began in 1848, **prospectors** headed west, hoping to strike it rich. Railroads were built to provide faster, easier **transportation** across the United States. Cowboys herded cattle across the Great Plains. Life in the Wild West was exciting and offered adventure and opportunity.

This book will take you back to this time in American history and will introduce you to eight different symbols of the Wild West. After you learn about the history behind the symbols, you will be able to draw a cartoon of each one by following six simple steps. Directions beneath each step will help you to add the new parts to your cartoon drawing. New steps are shown in red. A list of drawing terms and shapes is found on page 22.

Round up these supplies to draw cartoon symbols of the Wild West:

- Paper
- A sharp pencil or a felt-tipped marker
- An eraser
- Colored pencils or crayons to add color

To draw your cartoons, find a desk or a table in a quiet place. Make sure that you have enough light and that all your supplies are close by. To become a successful cartoonist, take your time and have fun!

Giddyap on over to the next page and have a rootin' tootin' good time drawing cartoon symbols of the Wild West!

The American Bison

American bison once grazed on grasslands from the Appalachian Mountains to the Rocky Mountains. The bison has a large head and neck and a hump over  its front shoulders. These areas are covered with thick, brown fur that forms a beard at the chin. The bison also has sharp, curved horns. It is about 6 feet (2 m) tall at its shoulders and weighs about 2,000 pounds (907 kg). In the mid-1800s, about 20 million bison lived in North America. Many Native Americans depended on bison for survival. They killed only what they needed. They ate the meat and used the hides to make clothing and shelter. They turned the horns and bones into tools. By the late 1800s, pioneers had killed millions of bison for sport. Fewer than 1,000 bison were left. Laws were made to protect the bison. Today about 200,000 bison roam on ranches and in national parks.

1

Start with the front of the head. Draw two curved lines. Make a backward letter C for the mouth. Add a straight line, two curved letter V's, and bumpy lines for fur.

2

Make a circle and smaller shaded circle for the eye. Add a bumpy line above it. Draw an upside-down, curved letter V with a bumpy line under it for the horn. Add a backward letter C and two dots for the nose.

3

You're a superstar! Make a bent line for the front of the leg. Add three lines and an upside-down letter V for the hoof. Make a long, bumpy line for fur.

4

Draw two bent lines for the body. Add two more for the back leg. Make straight lines for the hoof. Draw two bent lines with a bumpy line at the end for the tail.

5

Keep up the great work! Draw a curved line and a bumpy line for the second front leg. Make two curved lines for the back leg. Draw three lines and an upside-down letter V for each hoof.

6

Add detail and action lines on your bison. Draw grass. Make more bison and grass.

Railroads

Railroads helped to bring people to the Wild West. The first railroad in North America was the Baltimore-Ohio line. The first American steam **locomotive** ran on

this line. The 13-mile (21-km) line ran from Baltimore to Ellicott's Mills, Maryland, when it opened to the public in 1830. Soon more railroads were built. Merchants used railroads to move **freight**. The government used railroads to move pioneers to unsettled places. In 1848, the discovery of gold in California also helped the building of railroads. In the 1850s, as many as 2,000 miles (3,219 km) of train track were added per year. The first **transcontinental** railroad was finished in Promontory, Utah, on May 10, 1869. This 1,775-mile (2,857-km) railroad shortened travel time across the United States from many months to six days!

1

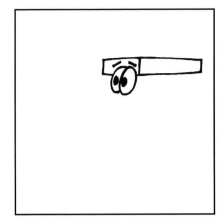

Choo choo! Draw an oval, a letter C, and two big dots for eyes. Add two straight lines for eyebrows. Make horizontal and vertical lines for the top of the train.

2

Next make a long, thin rectangle with short curved lines on each end. Draw two circle shapes for each wheel. Add straight lines inside the wheels for spokes.

3

Draw two vertical lines to connect the top to the wheels. Add a line between the wheels. Make a square window, and add vertical and angled lines. Draw a rectangle beneath it.

4

On the left side, make a small oval and write a number inside. Add two curved lines, two straight lines, and another curved line. Draw a smile and a line in front of the eyes.

5

Outstanding effort! Draw two vertical lines, two angled lines, two more vertical lines, and two slightly curved lines for the smokestack. Add bumpy lines for smoke. Make a light using a circle and straight lines. Add a bell.

6

Make the grate using straight lines and tilted rectangles. Draw the train track. All aboard!

The Pony Express

The Pony Express delivered mail between St. Joseph, Missouri, and Sacramento, California. It began on April 3, 1860, and continued until October 26, 1861. Regular mail delivery, by boat or stagecoach, took up to three weeks. The Pony

Express took 10 days. About 34,753 pieces of mail were delivered by the Pony Express. Riders on horseback carried mail in leather saddlebags over a 1,966-mile (3,164-km) trail. They stopped to change horses every 10 to 15 miles (16–24 km) at 1 of the 190 stations on the trail. New riders took over every 75 to 100 miles (121–161 km). Riders earned $100 per month. The fastest delivery made by the Pony Express, a copy of President Abraham Lincoln's first speech to Congress, took 7 days and 17 hours. The Pony Express stopped after the transcontinental **telegraph** began working on October 24, 1861.

1

Draw a curved line and a bent shape for the hat. Make a circle, a curved line, and dots for eyes. Add a nose, an ear, and hair. Make straight lines for the mouth and jaw.

2

Draw ovals for the bandanna. Make the shirt using straight lines. Add an oval belt buckle. Draw letter *U*'s for the hands. Add two curved lines and a short line for pants. Make the boot and stirrup using straight and curved lines.

3

Draw the horse's eyes. Add a bent line, a curved line, and a straight line for the nose. Make a bit and reins. Draw the jaw and neck. Add the ears and the mane.

4

Under the hands, make a circle and bent lines for the saddle. Add a line for the rider's other leg. Draw slightly curved lines, bent lines, and short lines for the front legs.

5

Draw a curved line for the back of the saddle, then add the top of the tail. Make zigzag lines and another curved line for the tail. Add a curved line, then bent lines for the back legs. Add the hooves. Finish the belly.

6

Add two rectangles, letter *V*'s and dots for the mailbags. Add action lines and detail.

11

Covered Wagons

Pioneers traveled west in covered wagons. Many pioneers traveled in groups of wagons called wagon trains. They moved from 10 to 15 miles (16–24 km)

per day. Many traveled in wagons called prairie **schooners**. These wagons were thought to look like boats, sailing across the prairie. Other wagons were named Conestoga wagons, for the Conestoga Valley in Pennsylvania where they were first built in the 1700s. Conestoga wagons were bigger than prairie schooners. They were used mostly to move goods. Covered wagons had a wooden frame made of hickory, oak, or maple. Four to seven wooden poles, called bows, were bent into hoops and covered with **canvas** to make the top. The canvas was rubbed with oil to make it **waterproof**. Large wheels kept the wagon from getting stuck in the mud. From two to eight horses, mules, or oxen pulled the wagon.

1

Yeehaa! Begin by drawing a circle and a letter C with two smaller, shaded circles for the eyes. Add two curved lines.

2

Next draw four lines and three curved lines for the top of the canvas. Make a long curved line for the back. Draw a long horizontal line on the bottom of the canvas.

3

Make two circles for each wheel. Add a small circle and a letter C in the center of each wheel. Make straight lines for spokes.

4

You are really talented! Make horizontal and vertical lines for the wooden wagon bottom.

5

I like your creativity! Add curved lines for the other wheels. Make straight lines for their spokes.

6

Draw the nose and the mouth. Add action lines and detail. Move 'em out!

The Native American Tepee

Native Americans, or American Indians, were the first people to live in North America. About 40 different Plains Indian groups lived in the western United States. For shelter, they built large, cone-shaped tents called tepees. They used three or

four poles tied together at the top and spread out at the bottom to make the frame. Lighter poles were added to support the tepee. To cover the frame, the women sewed from 14 to 20 bison hides together using **sinew** from bison muscle. The hides were wrapped around the frame and were held in place with wooden pegs. A hole at the top let smoke escape from the fire that always burned inside the tepee. The door was also made from bison hide or fur. The tepee was painted inside and outside with battle scenes or other designs.

1

Start by drawing an oval with a shaded oval inside for each eye. Add a letter *U* for the nose. Make a thick letter *U* with a short line at each end for the mouth.

2

Next draw two angled lines and a long wiggly line for the tepee. Add a short line between the eyes for the top.

3

Nice effort! Make four rectangles for poles at the top of the tepee.

4

Next draw two lines for each arm. Make five curved lines on each hand for fingers.

5

Make an upside-down, wiggly letter *V* for the door. Add angled lines for shading. Add a wiggly line with short lines across it to show sinew stitches above the door.

6

Add detail and designs. Draw action lines, smoke, and the ground. Make another tepee!

15

Cowboys

The first cowboys in the Wild West lived in Texas. From the 1860s to the 1880s, they **herded** millions of cattle across the open range for ranch owners. Cowboys moved from 2,000 to 3,000 cattle about 1,000 miles (1,609 km) at a time on trail drives. It took from two to three months to herd the

cattle to railroad stations. The cattle were then sent to the East Coast, where they were sold for $40 to $50 each. During roundups in the spring and the fall, cowboys brought the cattle to the ranch and **branded** the newborn calves. Each ranch had its own brand. Cowboys often worked on horseback. They used ropes called **lariats** to catch cattle. They wore hats with wide brims to keep the sun off their faces, and bandannas to keep dust out of their mouths. They also wore leather **chaps** over their pants to protect their legs, and boots with pointed toes.

1

Draw a circle, a letter *C*, and dots for the eyes. Make curved lines for the nose, jaw, and ear. Add two thick bent lines for the mustache, and a shaded oval for the mouth.

2

Make a bent shape for the brim of the hat. Complete the hat by making an upside-down letter *U*, a straight line, and two curved lines. Shade in the hair.

3

Make a curved letter *V*, a circle, teardrops, and lines for the bandanna. Draw six lines and one dot for each shirtsleeve. Make two curved lines and a short line for the body.

4

Next make curved lines for the hands and fingers. Add letter *U*'s and wavy lines for the lariat. Draw short lines on the lariat.

5

Splendid! Make a wide letter *U* for the belt buckle and two curved lines for the belt. Add a curved line to finish the shirt. Draw bumpy lines for the outside of the chaps. Finish them with a straight line and two bent lines.

6

Make two wavy lines, two ovals, and lines to finish the lariat. Add action lines. Draw grass and cattle.

Lawmen

As frontier towns grew, so did the need for lawmen. Many towns had problems with **crime**. **Outlaws**, or bandits, stole gold and silver by **ambushing** wagons or **stagecoaches** and by robbing banks. Claim jumpers took mine claims that didn't belong to them. **Rustlers** stole cattle and changed their brands.

Sheriffs and federal marshals worked to keep law and order in frontier towns. Wyatt Earp was a marshal in Tombstone, Arizona. He is remembered for his bravery in a gunfight with outlaws at the O.K. Corral. Bass Reeves was another famous lawman. He was one of the Wild West's first African American deputy marshals. The Texas Rangers also protected pioneers and kept the towns safe. Groups of townspeople sometimes got together to punish criminals. These groups were called **vigilantes**.

18

1

Start with a letter *U* for the head. Draw curved lines and dots for the ears. Shade in the hair. Make a long curved line and an upside-down letter *U* for the hat.

2

Terrific! Make two circles and two dots for the eyes. Draw a letter *U* for the nose. Shade in an upside-down letter *U* for the mustache. Draw a straight line and a letter *U* for the mouth. Shade it in.

3

Make three lines for each sleeve. Draw six more lines for the rest of the coat. Add two curved lines on each side for the collar. Draw a star for your lawman's badge.

4

Make the shirt with letter *U*'s, a circle, two upside-down hearts, and a line. Make four lines and an oval for the belt. Draw straight and curved lines for the cuffs and hands.

5

Make straight lines to draw the pantlegs. Draw a curved, sideways letter *V* and three short lines for each boot. Add a straight line and a letter *X* for each spur.

6

Make a bank and a jail using straight lines. Add detail, action lines, and a cloud. Nice work!

19

The Gold Rush

On January 24, 1848, James Marshall discovered gold in California. He was building a sawmill for John Sutter along the American River. Sutter tried to keep Marshall's discovery a secret, but

word spread and the gold rush began. Gold miners panned for gold by scooping dirt or gravel into shallow pans. When they held the pans under running water, the water washed away the dirt and gravel. The gold was heavier and stayed in the bottom of the pan. Miners used axes, shovels, and picks to dig into the ground. In 1849, almost $10 million worth of gold was mined in California. The miners became known as the forty-niners. By 1853, about 200,000 gold seekers had come to California from all over the United States, Europe, Australia, and even from China! Only a few of them became rich from gold.

1

Start by making a circle, a letter C, and two shaded circles for the eyes. Make a curved line for the nose. Draw bumpy lines for the mustache and the beard.

2

Draw a long, curved shape for the brim of the hat. Add two curved lines for the top of the hat. Make a short line above the left eye. Shade in a mouth. Add a backward letter C and a dot for the ear.

3

You did it! Make a straight line, a curved line, and a rectangle for the shirtsleeve. Draw two lines for the wrist. Add five letter U's for the fingers.

4

You are a super artist! Make straight lines for the shirt and the second shirtsleeve. Draw a bent line and a letter U for the hand. Add curved lines for the pan.

5

Draw a backward letter C for the belt buckle. Add a square and two rectangles to complete the belt. Make straight and bent lines for the pants.

6

Add detail, gold nuggets, and action lines. Draw a stream, rocks, a pick, grass, and a caption.

Terms for Drawing Cartoons

Here are some of the words and shapes you'll use to draw cartoon symbols of the Wild West:

Action lines   Letter *V*

Angled lines   Letter *X*

Bent lines   Oval

Bumpy line   Rectangle

Circle   Square

Curved line   Straight lines

Detail   Teardrop

Dots   Thick line

Horizontal line   Vertical line

Letter *C*   Zigzag line

Letter *U*

Glossary

ambushing (AM-bush-ing) Attacking by surprise from a hiding place.

branded (BRAND-id) Marked with a design burned on by a hot iron pole.

canvas (KAN-ves) A strong cloth with a coarse weave, often made of cotton.

chaps (CHAPS) Leather material worn over pants by cowboys to protect their legs.

crime (KRYM) An act that breaks the law.

freight (FRAYT) Goods carried by train, wagon, or boat to merchants or customers.

frontier (frun-TEER) The edge of a settled country, where the wilderness begins.

herded (HURD-ed) Gathered and moved animals.

lariats (LAR-ee-uts) Long ropes with a loop at the end, used to catch livestock.

locomotive (loh-kuh-MOH-tiv) The first train car that pulls the rest of the cars.

opportunities (ah-per-TOO-nih-teez) Good chances.

outlaws (OWT-lawz) People who have broken the law and are on the run from the law.

pioneers (py-uh-NEERZ) Some of the first people to settle in a new area.

prospectors (PRAH-spek-terz) People who explore an area for minerals, such as gold.

rustlers (RUS-lurz) Thieves, especially those who steal animals from farms or ranches.

schooners (SKOO-nerz) Fast, sturdy boats with two masts.

sinew (SIN-yoo) A strong band of living tissue that joins muscle to bone.

stagecoaches (STAYJ-kohch-ez) Coaches, pulled by horses, that carried passengers and mail from stop to stop.

telegraph (TEH-lih-graf) A machine used to send messages through air waves using coded signals.

transcontinental (tranz-kon-tin-EN-tul) Going across a continent.

transportation (tranz-per-TAY-shun) A way of traveling from one place to another.

vigilantes (vih-jih-LAN-teez) People who take the law into their own hands to punish lawbreakers.

waterproof (WAH-ter-proof) Not able to get wet.

Index

Web Sites

Due to the changing nature of Internet links, PowerKids Press has developed an online list of Web sites related to the subject of this book. This site is updated regularly. Please use this link to access the list:
www.powerkidslinks.com/kgd/wildwest/